Contents

List of Illustrations

Preface

I am a submariner. I have a love of the sea and the depths of the oceans. The thrill of operations at sea and a love of my country are what keep me motivated to leave the land and ones I love for months of isolation. In the course of my career, I have had the privilege to serve under some of the best men and leaders I have known. At the same time, I have served under some that do not honor the men they serve. Through my training of many young submariners, I have had the opportunity to listen to and understand some of the frustrations we each have shared as a result of both the good and the bad of leaders. The frequency at which the toxic leaders emerge is the concern that I have and the effect that they have on both the direction of the submarine force and the quality of the junior officers that we retain. This concern is the driving force behind this paper. The content is reflective of 10 years of listening to other officers wishing something would be done about it. I would like to thank ACSC and Lieutenant Colonel Brian Landry for the inspiration and opportunity to voice the concerns and solutions that are presented in this paper.

Abstract

Utilizing the problem-solution format, this research paper explores the effects of leadership styles in the U.S. submarine force that have perpetuated from its inception and the effects that they have on the operational effectiveness of the submarine crews. It explores the effects of Admiral Hyman G. Rickover's leadership style and how the emphasis on nuclear power has reduced the operational effectiveness of today's force. Additionally, the paper explores the difference between apparent and actual leadership training in the submarine force and how a focus on technical acumen over tactics and leadership has created an environment where toxic leadership styles can flourish. Two case studies are used to analyze the effects of toxic leadership on submarine crews along with the example of one leader that was able to make a significant impact for one crew in the midst of a toxic leader.

This paper finds that the current leadership training model and focus is insufficient for the needs of up-and-coming commanding officers. It recommends implementation of two integrated solutions that would ensure we remain the premier subsurface navy in the world. First, we must implement a focus on servant-leadership with a corresponding increase in training time allotted in training schools. This focus must continue through the subsequent tours of duty at sea. Second, a change in the officer career pipeline is recommended to split the officer corps into either tactical officers or technical officers. This would allow officer career fields that focus on operational employment of the submarine and engineering separately.

Leadership in Command under the Sea

Command at sea is the pinnacle of the submarine naval officer's career. It is a time when the submarine officer becomes the tip of the war fighting spear. The mantel of submarine command brings with it a weight of responsibility that few will ever understand. Nowhere in society is one man responsible for every detail of human life to the extent of that a submarine captain. The production of water, the production of oxygen for breathing, the removal of all atmosphere contaminants, the storage and production of food for several months, the health and medical needs, and the safety of each man in the most hostile of environments. His command platform is "filled from one end to the other inside with 450 volts of electrical generators, equipment and wires, 4500 pound air pressure systems, and 3000 pound hydraulic oil."[1] All this and more rests upon the shoulders of the submarine commanding officer in the confines of a 360' ship amongst the most awesome firepower known to mankind with a several hundred Watt nuclear reactor at bone crushing depths that are in excess of 800' and 350 psi. Encased in this pressure vessel, the commanding officer takes his crew and massive platform of kinetic and potential energy into enemy waters under presidential tasking on orders higher than top secret to perform tasks and collect information vital to national security. This must be done for periods of six months or longer while keeping the moral of the crew high while confined to living quarters smaller than a walk-in closet.[2] This only begins to shed light on the burden of leadership that rests upon the shoulders of a United States Navy Submarine Commanding Officer.

It is no wonder then that under such extreme pressures we develop very talented, technically minded professionals. However, under those same stresses and pressures, we develop extremes in leadership styles and abilities. With all that is placed on these men in their training and preparation to take such a technologically advanced weapon into such hostile

1

environments, we fail to give them the proper training in leadership and experience necessary to ensure that each commanding officer is successful. I attribute this partially to an insufficient focus on leadership training and employment through the officer career path. The other part, I attribute to a leadership style perpetuated by the father of the nuclear submarine community, Admiral Hyman G. Rickover, who personally selected each of his nuclear officers.

Considering all the risks involved, it is understandable why the focus of the submarine officer's training pipeline focuses primarily on the technical first and then the tactical second. Additionally, submarine commanders perform their tasks under the strong influence of the Naval Reactors nuclear umbrella. This leads to a technically minded corps of officers that overemphasizes technical acumen over tactical acumen. "Michael Dobbs, a former submarine CO said, 'The emphasis on engineering over war fighting and mariner skills during the submarine officer's formative years can ingrain an overly strong reliance on analytical decision-making that often lasts an entire career. Officers are indoctrinated into a mindset where facts, precedent, and strict adherence to procedures dominate intuition, common sense, and what feels right.'"[3] "The submarine force's preoccupation with being 'good nukes' is the bedrock of its risk-averse culture and is at the heart of its protective controlling nature. For the past 60 years, the force has trained tomorrow's leaders to be nuclear engineers first, naval tacticians and strategists second."[4] The purpose of this narrative study is to understand the leadership model in the United States submarine force, how it diminishes operational effectiveness, and how implementation of two integrated solutions would ensure we remain the premier subsurface navy.

Background

Rickover's Influence

In order to understand the problems with the leadership model that permeates the submarine force, one must understand its beginning and background. The submarine force has a rich and vibrant history full of stories of honor and prestige from World War II to present day. Throughout those many years, there have been significant changes in the submarine force. The force started out as a diesel-electric boat fleet that spent more time on the surface than submerged. This all changed with the advent of nuclear power and Admiral Hyman G. Rickover, the father of our Nuclear Navy.

Admiral Rickover immigrated to the United States from Poland with his parents just prior to WWI. He was an extremely driven, focused man that found little use for relaxation or personal pleasure. As a junior naval officer, he was made a Department Head as the Engineer on his first ship due to his drive and meticulous nature. Seeing the future on naval warfare in the submarine force, he transitioned to submarines with the express vision of nuclear power carrying these machines to the extreme. It was through his vision, drive and determination that the advent of the nuclear submarine came to fruition. The process of getting approval for this nuclear submarine force and maintaining it was not an easy one. This rested on the shoulders of Hyman G. Rickover for the majority of his 63 year naval career, serving longer than any other admiral in naval history. In 1946 Rickover pushed his way into a position at Oak Ridge National Laboratories on the heels of the Manhattan Project.[5] This would be the beginnings of Naval Reactors and his leadership in the force. He had a clear vision for nuclear power and what it could do for the nation. His vision and direction was so crucial that the attempted forced retirement of Rickover by several other Navy admirals was blocked on many occasions by four different presidents. Why did so many want his retirement on so many different occasions when he was the one that led so much innovation? It was due to the way in which he did it. His leadership style was one of tyrannical control. A 1954 time magazine article stated, "Sharp-tongued Hyman Rickover spurred his men to exhaustion, ripped through red tape, and drove contractors into rages."[6] His temper and tongue it seemed were in constant battle as to which could be the hottest and sharpest. Even the most accomplished and personally selected to work for him had conflicting feelings. Such was the case with Edward L. Beach, Jr., who worked as his right hand man for many years and referred to "the kindly old gentleman" (or simply "KOG", as Rickover became euphemistically known in inner circles) unaffectionately as a "tyrant" with "no account of his gradually failing powers" in his later years.[7]

When the question from congress came as to how he would ensure that his program did not have any mistakes, Rickover responded that he would personally choose each officer that came into the Naval Nuclear Engineering program. This he did by personally interviewing each Nuclear Propulsion Officer Candidate in his office after they passed a series of technical oral interviews and written examinations.[8] This process continues today. The means by which he would test candidates were bizarre in many senses. In an interview with Diane Sawyer of CBS' 60 Minutes, he admitted to "locking candidates in broom closets…, making them sit in chairs during the interview with the two front legs cut off…, insulting them personally," and a myriad of other strange tactics.[9] This was his way of screening those that were the right type to watch over his nuclear reactors. It is no wonder then that many of the officers he chose only emulated the example of their highest leader, the one that directed the nuclear navy.

Admiral Rickover and his successors had a significant impact on the personality and direction of the submarine force. It is important to know that the admiral over all the U.S. submarine force is a three star. Admiral Rickover and his successors at Naval Reactors are all four star admirals.[10] This technical force has the power and has many times exercised it to remove a submarine from the active force when they deem the crew to be not competent in their ability to operate the reactor plant. The Rickover mentality has permeated throughout the ages and every level of operations of the submarine force. It has been both a blessing and a curse. While it has provided a history and atmosphere of zero defects, it has placed an emphasis on the technical nature of the submarines and a focus on nuclear power vice tactics and leadership.[11] Coupled with the aforementioned pressures of command at sea and the abrasive leadership style taught by example of these early leaders, some of our submarine commanding officers develop toxic leadership styles once the hatch is shut and the ship is submerged. Leadership analyst Gillian Flynn defines a toxic leader as one "who bullies, threatens, yells. The manager whose mood swings determine the climate of the office on any given day. They succeed by tearing others down."[12] This is the type of leader and commanding officer that should have no place in our submarine force. Unfortunately, we not only allow it but secretly condone it at times. How is it then that these types of leaders are still developed and advanced? It is due to our culture from the Rickover mentality and culture is a difficult element to change.

The Making of a Submarine Commanding Officer

"Being the commanding officer of a U.S. submarine, is one of the most prized and competitively sought jobs in the Navy. The Navy begins grooming prospective submarine commanders from the moment they are commissioned as ensigns–hoping to make each sub captain careful but decisive, reliant but not dependent on his crew"[13] It is in the initial training that the leadership styles of Rickover and his successors are ingrained in the minds and personalities of young officers. Since every commanding officer must be nuclear qualified as established by Rickover at the birth of the program, the road to command commences with the technical nuclear training.[14] A submarine officer's first exposure to the submarine force is through Rickover's strong nuclear training program that engulfs their lives for the first year and a half of training. In this nuclear training pipeline, the newly commissioned officer receives only one week of leadership training. After passing nuclear power school, nuclear prototype and the Submarine Basic Officer Course, Ensigns report to their first submarine. The first two years onboard are focused on nuclear propulsion and preparation for certification by Naval Reactors as Engineer. The training is intense with little time for sleep and virtually no relaxation. It is only in the last six to nine months left onboard that the officers focus on tactics and ship driving.

Technical Versus Tactical

Which is more important, to be technically or tactically proficient? In theory the submarine community wants a balance between the two. In reality, the facts show the opposite. The training pipeline for the junior officer shows a 1 to 4 ratio for tactical versus technical training.[15] Granted, this is in the first seven years of commissioned service and tactical training does increase starting with the eighth year. The focus for the crew underway does not change though. My experience with two submarines and working with the officers and crews from around the fleet highlights an overwhelming feeling that the purpose of the submarine is to transport the nuclear reactor around the seas. Underway, the typical submarine will drill four days a week. Three of those days are spent entirely with propulsion/nuclear plant related drills while the fourth day will be dedicated to drills forward of the reactor plant and tactical scenarios. If ship's schedule does not allow for all four drill sets that week, the first set to be removed will typically be the tactical set. The justification is due to a minimum number of hours of casualty training drills that Naval Reactors requires each quarter.

Commanding officers fear failure of not meeting the quota of drills and evolutions required of Naval Reactors each quarter. In fact, each commanding officer is required to submit a detailed nuclear training report to the head of Naval Reactors each quarter.[16] This report details every hour of classroom training, evolution, and problems encountered with each group of nuclear trained individuals aboard ship, especially the officers. I have seen on several occasion messages that directed my commanding officers to call Naval Reactors and explain the contents of one of these letters. On the other end of the scale, there is no similar report that details an equivalent tactical training process for the crew or officers. One of the driving factors is the requirement for the ship to pass an Operational Reactors Safeguard Exam (ORSE) every year, regardless of the condition of the ship. The requirement is not as stringent on the tactical side. Additionally, failure to pass the ORSE is grounds to have "the keys"[17] taken away from the commanding officer where failure of a Tactical Readiness Exam (TRE) does not yield the same result. This umbrella of nuclear influence permeates every aspect of life aboard ship. It is what makes us the safest among all disciplines in the Navy.[18] However, the focus that is placed upon safe operations of nuclear power has forced the submarine force to be more concerned with the technical vice tactical. This unbalance has placed us in second place in the world's eyes in submarine tactical ability to the British whose tactical training in their Perisher Command Course is considered the premier training program for submariners around the world.[19]

The few U.S. submariners that are privileged to attend the course each year return astounded at the difference in focus and training between the U.S. and our British counterparts. Many of the tactics, thumb rules, and litany that we now employ come from the training that

U.S. submarine officers learn while at Perisher. It is clear that the U.S. is still on the forefront of technical development of submarine platforms but has lost the edge in the tactical training for the employment of them due to a disproportionate focus on nuclear power.

We must not lose sight of the ultimate goal in our training. It is the ability to safely employ the most technically advanced submarines with tactical superiority.[20] Commander Ryan Ramsey of the Royal Navy stated, "The ultimate goal for those that contribute to the progression of the Junior Warfare Officer (JWO) is to produce a Commanding Officer, capable of great warfare feats, able to lead his team effectively with authority and manage the demanding administrative workings of a submarine. Making the submarine JWO develop from the analytical approach to leadership and decision making to the intuitive approach is what should be achieved prior to his Department Head tour - it is possible! Tactics, guidelines and experience play a significant part in the intuitive approach." This is not the case in the U.S. submarine force. The focus on tactics for officer development does not begin until the Department Head tour. One of the premier U.S. submarine tacticians Captian Emil Casciano stated, "Intuitive decisions are made after one detects cues and patterns that emerge from complex situations, and then chooses a course of action that likely will be successful. The action chosen is based on experience-the person has seen similar situations and draws on a 'library' of responses."[21] If we are not giving adequate time to the junior officers to develop a bank of experiences to pull from, then the intuitive decisions that Captain Casciano speaks of will not be intuitive and mistakes will be made.

Submarine Officer Leadership Model

During the thirty to thirty-three month initial sea tour, each officer is assigned to various divisions as the division officer with a chief petty officer to teach him how to be a division officer. The experiences that an officer has as a leader in these division officer billets are as varied as the individuals. Some do receive excellent opportunities to step up and lead while others are told by the chief to just work on getting qualified and let him worry about the division. The opportunity to lead is significant, but not all take advantage of the opportunity. The officers that do take advantage of the opportunity become the cream of the crop and are the reason "that they are highly sought, for positions in career fields outside the nuclear power industry."[22] Sadly, it is many of the "good ones that get out" according to a consensus on the Navy First Class Petty Officer leadership forum.[23]

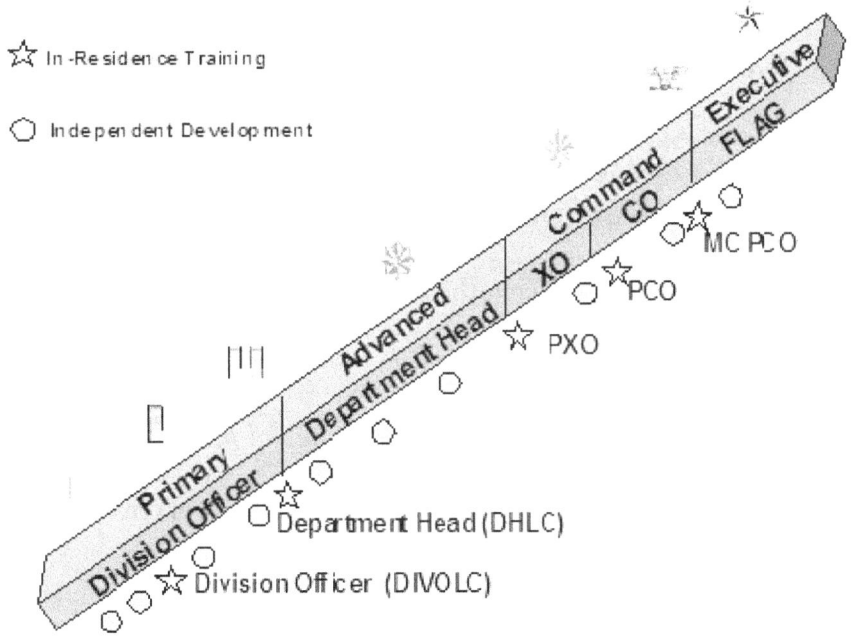

Figure 1. Officer Leadership Development Continuum

This lack of leadership training continues as officers progress through Department Head, Executive Officer, and finally, Commanding Officer. As seen in figure 1, the submarine officer corps only receives one week of formal leadership instruction prior to each assignment.[24] This training is esteemed by many as another week of vacation since it generally follows several months of intense technical or tactical training.[25] A focus on leadership training and application is generally non-existent in the training pipeline though the models show the contrary.[26] This mentality is permeated by many in the training facilities and in the community. Hence many believe that leadership is something that is learned on the job. This "lack in frequency of leadership training and the less than adequate professional training means that the brunt of the shortfall must be made up by mentorship at the unit level."[27] The issue is that it is Rickover's toxic, micro-management style of leadership that is generally adopted to fill the void of training since that is what many officers see and experience. The problem becomes one of incorporating "the wrong mentorship, (thus) a cycle of poor leaders and submariners are generated. Once this starts it is very difficult to break."[28]

Leadership Effects on Retention

The result is the loss of talent from year to year as the "good" officers leave since they feel that they cannot make a difference or endure the oppressive environment.[29] As one officer stated in his resignation letter, "The most significant problem I see is our continual use of negative leadership. My decision to resign is based primarily on my experiences with the quality of leadership. I believe that poor leadership is, in fact, the source of much of the discontent that I see in most of my peers. It is not simply an issue of an unpleasant encounter with one or several individuals. Instead, my experiences and observations are evidence of a leadership culture that is fundamentally flawed."[30] Numerous examples of resignations that site leadership as the number one problem fill the internet although in my experience, many of the junior officer's removed any language about poor leadership practices prior to submission. The primary reason that many do this is due to the repercussions and many interviews that followed when their peers submitted letters citing leadership reasons. This could explain why a study of U.S. Navy junior officer retention found "that leadership has not been a significant factor in submarine officer retention."[31] While there is an impressive corps of officers that do stay and assume command, the atmosphere is prime for those that develop toxic leadership traits to stay and continue the cycle of screamers, as they are commonly referred to amongst the ranks.[32]

Retention is a problem in the submarine officer corps and has been for the last three decades.[33] Vice Admiral N. R. Ryan, Chief of Naval Personnel, stated before the Subcommittee on Personnel of the Senate Armed Services Committee on Recruiting/Retention in February 2000, "Retaining the right quantity and quality of nuclear-trained officers remains the primary challenge for the community. Submarine officer retention is currently below that required to sustain force structure. Retention rates improved in FY99 to 30 percent (compared to FY98 retention of 27 percent). Retention rates must improve to a nominal 38 percent to adequately meet steady-state manning requirements."[34] The submarine force has not met this goal and retention hovers from year to year just below the 38 percent mark.[35]

Is the job not challenging enough? Is the pay not sufficient? Is it the time away from home? The answer to those three questions is a resounding no.[36] It goes without saying that the job is extremely challenging. The pay is the best in all of the military.[37] A Navy submarine O-3 with six years time in service makes on average $120,000 a year with bonuses and subpay.[38] The Nuclear Officer Incentive Bonus was recently approved to be raised from $25,000 to $30,000 per year.[39] The job is difficult aboard a submarine. Time away from family is a heavy burden to bear. However, these are not the main reasons that our quality officers get out. It is due to the toxic atmosphere that some leaders in the submarine community create. Otherwise, we would not have to throw the tens of thousands a year in bonuses and submarine pay at each officer in an attempt to retain them. Retention rates have not increased as the bonuses have increased over the years.[40] Money is not the answer. The right type of leadership is.

Toxic Leadership

No leader is going to be perfect and please all his subordinates. Mistakes will always be made as decisions are not always black and white, right or wrong. Leaders will have to make decisions at times that are unpopular, difficult to enforce and possibly lead to loss of life. Many organizations and particularly the different branches of the armed forces deal with counterproductive leadership styles that emerge with new leaders and situations. The concern becomes of what will be the long lasting effects on the unit from poor leadership. Organizations can and do recover from poor leadership. The leadership style in question here is not poor leadership but toxic leadership. In Military Review of July 2004, Colonel George E. Reed, U.S. Army, analyzed the problem with toxic leadership and why it continues in the military. He concluded that "military culture esteems technical competence, and technical competence will lead some senior leaders to overlook flawed toxic leaders."[41] Additionally, "subordinates might not report toxic leaders because nobody likes a whiner. We expect professionals to perform to the best of their ability despite a supervisor's leadership style."[42] In the military, we have a tendency to just grin and bear it with the knowledge that changes in command come every few years. Hence it is easier to wait out toxic leaders."[43] Exacerbating the problem is that these leaders continue to progress in the system and "the higher they progress, the more damage they do."[44]

While attending the Air War College (AWC), Colonel Reed reported that "virtually every AWC student participating in the project could speak about serving under toxic leaders."[45] The submarine force is no different. If anything, we develop them in greater numbers and toxicity due to the emphasis on nuclear technical competence and lack of leadership training. This coupled with the intense operations at sea in the confines of the submarine only accentuate toxic leadership characteristics. There is much evidence that supports the fact that toxic leaders continue to develop and progress throughout the submarine force. Occasionally these leaders' effects don't stay hidden beneath the depths of the oceans but surface to the point that they are relieved of command. This happened most recently on the USS WEST VIRGINIA, as the commanding officer "was relieved due to a loss of confidence in his ability to command."[46] Although there were no specific incidents that led to his relief, it was due to the poor command climate that he fostered.[47] Several forums discuss the specifics from the crew underway, many of which cannot be validated. The fact is though that when the toxicity of the commanding officer reaches the levels that they are relieved, the command climate and moral of the crew is damaged to the point that it will take years to recover. This is not an isolated incident as several submarine commanding officers have been relieved over the years for similar issues. The two cases that follow are of toxic leaders, submarine commanders, one which was relieved of command and the other was not.

Leadership Case Studies

USS FLORIDA 1997

In July 1997, the commander of the USS FLORIDA was relieved of command due to loss of confidence.[48] The commander was a prior enlisted officer. The crew knew this and was excited to have him aboard when he took command since they felt that his command style would reflect the experience of being "one of them."[49] One of the Chief Petty Officers said that the enlisted were especially excited since they "felt he knew what it was like to be on the deckplates."[50] This all changed once he took command and the hatches were shut with the submarine underway. Immediately the crew began to experience the wrath and public outbursts from the man that they looked to as their leader. Meals in the wardroom turned from being a time that the officers looked forward to for comradery and relaxation to a painful and awkward hour. On one occasion, when the commander was late for a meal, the executive officer (XO) borrowed the fork from the CO's place setting to replace one that was missing from his own. The XO thought it was alright since the CO was never late to a meal. When the CO later showed for the meal and saw his fork was gone, he lashed out at the XO, who had already apologized. "Don't you ever take my f---ing fork! It's my fork—don't touch it."[51] One of the junior officer lieutenants, who was sitting nearby, reported, "It was like a blast of a stage five hurricane."[52]

This was the first in a string of incidents that continued to escalate over the course of the patrol. Bursts of outrage and public humiliation were common. The crew reported that "few could hide from the skipper's wrath."[53] During an incident when the ship was at periscope depth with very high seas and the Diving Officer of the Watch was having difficulty maintaining depth, as expected for the conditions, the commanding officer "looked at him and announced loudly: 'You're disqualified."[54] The news of the incident shook the crew. The old adage, praise in public and reprimand in private was reversed. Many more similar incidences followed which only alienated the crew from the commanding officer. This is a dangerous situation. Once the crew is alienated, they won't tell the commanding officer of problems, they wait until the crisis hits. One of the crew reported, "You're not supposed to be afraid of your captain, to tell him stuff. But nobody wanted to."[55]

The culmination came during a Tactical Readiness Exam when many of admiral's staff heard the reports from the crew and reported up that the crew was "despondent."[56] Upon return to port, the group admiral gathered the facts and made the decision. The Commanding Officer was relieved of command. The official reports will often soften the actual conditions and stresses that the crew faced, as I have seen from personal experience. Fortunately, in this case the admiral believed his staff and took the reports seriously showing the moral courage that is needed to weed out this type of toxic leadership. Such was not the case in the next case study.

First Commanding Officer

During my tour as a Junior Officer on my first submarine, I served under one of these toxic leaders. My first captain was one that brought terror and fear wherever he went. His mere presence intimidated, and not out of respect. He was notorious for his horrible temper, his bursts of outrage, his demeaning and tearing apart of individuals in public, and the extremes that he would take in belittling even the most competent individual in front of his peers. Those that served with me under his tyrannical control in those dark days still tell others that there is no way that you could understand how utterly depressing and difficult it was. Even now, when those I come in contact with in senior navy leadership that knew him, find out that he was my first captain, they respond the same. "I can't believe that you stayed in the navy after serving under that man!" Unfortunately, it was not until his last patrol as commanding officer that he was investigated by the squadron. Interviews were held and many on the crew voiced their opinion and experiences. After a month of investigation, no changes were made. One source from the squadron told me and the other officers that the reason that he was not relieved was due to the fact that his scheduled change of command was only two months after the investigation. He said that the commodore felt it was better to just let him transfer and avoid the public embarrassment. We do know that he was issued a letter of instruction, a formal reprimand and instruction to change, for his actions but that was not sufficient. The moral courage to relieve him was not exhibited. Similarly, we as a crew failed to bring out many of the incidents early enough in his career to facilitate a change. We cowered in fear of what it would mean if we were the whiners that reported him.

The Example

However, it was while serving under such a leader that I learned one of the greatest lessons in the Navy and in life from another leader. It was the third strategic nuclear deterrent patrol that I had been on with this commanding officer and it was the worst. It was however the first one with my new executive officer, who was different in every way. It was on a particularly difficult day that the XO called the entire wardroom of officers together after the captain had went to bed. He not only saw the pain that the crew was under but had experienced it firsthand. It was there in that meeting that he asked the pointed question to all of us, "Men, why are we here?" There was a myriad of responses, most superficial in nature given the mood and a couple of cynical ones. The XO finally told us in so many words that though many of our responses had value, none of them were correct. He went on to say, "The reason we are here is to lead men!" Simple as it sounds, that answer gave us more direction and purpose than anything else could have. Why? Because it came from a man that did just that; he led men. He then set forth a pattern on how to lead the crew without undermining the captain. He inspired and cared for everyman on the ship which produced outstanding results, even though the attitude of the captain never changed. Until that patrol, we had not seen true leadership. It was the one thing we lacked until he stepped foot onboard. He taught each of us from that point on how to lead, even when those above us wouldn't or couldn't. He led from the front and united the crew without overriding or alienating the commanding officer. I didn't recognize it then but I do now. His style of leadership was one of servant leadership.

With the frequency of toxic leadership that is encountered in the submarine force, what can be done to eliminate it? Additionally, with the focus on the technical aspect of submarining over the tactical, what solutions are there to correct both problems? Correcting the problems now will not be easy but it must be done. The "submarine force leadership must embrace a new mindset that breaks with the culture that has developed over the past 60 years and promote the innovation, leadership and ingenuity that started with its World War II submarine heroes."[57] I pose two possible solutions, in the order of precedence; implement a focus on Servant Leadersip and change the officer career pipeline.

The Solutions

Time for Change: Servant Leadership in the Submarine Force

The first order of business is [to begin] on a course toward people-building with leadership that has a firmly established context of people first. With that, the right actions fall naturally into place.

—Robert K. Greenleaf

One junior officer that resigned after his initial commitment was completed stated, "The Navy's method of leadership is fundamentally based upon negative reinforcement. At every turn, behavioral change is attempted through criticism and punishment. As a junior officer first starting to monitor maintenance practices on my submarine, I was instructed by my Department Head to omit positive comments since they 'provided no value.' In the absence of negative comments, a simple disclaimer is made: 'No deficiencies noted.' Seldom is feedback provided highlighting what was done correctly or how to correct the deficiencies that were observed, and any such feedback is off the record."[58] An organization that focuses strictly on the negative will never achieve its full potential. A common saying among the submarine community is that you get what you inspect. Thus the tendency is a push to inspect and micro-manage everything. "If

17

we believe that responsible leaders must have their hands in everything, controlling every decision, person, and moment, then we cannot hope for anything except what we already have—a treadmill of frantic efforts that end up destroying our individual and collective vitality."[59] Servant-leadership can change this without sacrificing the outstanding safety record that the United States Submarine Force has earned and maintained throughout the years.

So what is servant-leadership? As Robert K. Greenleaf states, "The servant-leader is servant first… It begins with the natural feeling that one wants to serve, to serve first. Then conscious choice brings one to aspire to lead."[60] More appropriate, "a servant leader is an individual who aspires to serve first and espouses servant leadership theory not only in belief, but in action."[61] The transition from belief to consistent actions is the key to make servant-leadership valid. "Servant-leadership offers new ways to capitalize on the knowledge and wisdom of all…and encourages individuals to grow from just doing a job into having fully engaged minds and hearts."[62] It is a leadership style that is counterintuitive at first to the natural man, who inherently wants to control and direct with the sole purpose of results. Servant-leadership is a "holistic approach to work, building a sense of community, and the sharing of power in decision making."[63] It is not management by committee, or in our case, command by committee. Rather, it is the serving of those that one leads and, in the process, empowering them to act.

Why is this so important for the submarine force? It is due to the fact that each man that wears the coveted dolphins on his chest depends on each other for his life, in every action he takes aboard the submarine. Each valve, switch, or lever he operates, if done improperly, could cost the life of every man on the submarine. After months and years of training and upon earning the submarine dolphins, the commanding officer personally pins the dolphins on the newly qualified submariner and states, "Having my full confidence and trust…." Similarly, each man on the submarine must look at the captain and mentally state, "Having my full confidence and trust…" Submarining is inherently a symbiotic community by nature, each man depending on the other for his life and well being. The benefit of servant-leadership is the strength it brings by "encouraging everyone to actively seek opportunities to both serve and lead others, thereby setting up the potential for raising the quality of life throughout."[64]

So if this is the case, isn't servant leadership being employed already? The answer is yes and no. It is in a few isolated cases and by individuals that bring the practice with them with their natural feeling to want to serve, as was the case with my second Executive Officer. The majority do not, especially in today's society that does not focus on service of one another. The key is that "in the practice of servant-leadership, people confront their weaknesses, their egos, and their limitations, and are so empowered to deal with them."[65] Thus in confronting their weaknesses and egos, the leaders find humility, insight and understanding. It forces them to understand more of the situations that they will deal with and remove their own personal biases out of the decision making process. The result is that the crew and those they serve will feel that that commanding officer truly has their best interest at the core of his heart while fulfilling the requirements of the mission. "When servant-leadership becomes a goal of the organization---or part of its vision---those who adopt it become mentors to each other. Learners are thus apprenticed to mentors but also to one another."[66] This in return leads to greater confidence in the abilities of the subordinate and a desire for excellence in every aspect. A cycle thus begins that only elevates the entire crew and it becomes infectious.

In the process of implementing servant-leadership as the standard for leadership in the submarine force, it is important that the men understand that a servant leader is not a weak leader. Servant leaders in the submarine force inherently need to be decisive individuals, strong in their abilities, just not overbearing or belittling. It is incumbent on a servant leader to inspire by their example and to not make their subordinates cower or act out of fear. Command is a position, leadership is not.[67] Why are we here? "To lead men!" This should be the mindset of every commissioned officer in the submarine force. We are not meant to be the technical experts, but the tactical experts that lead and fight the ship. If that is to be the case, we must inspire those that work for us. The question then becomes how. In the submarine force, knowledge generally brings respect. We must be knowledgeable in the technical aspects, but we are not meant to be the experts. We must learn to lead in a way that inspires. The practice "begins with serving, not because it is more important than leading, but because it is more difficult."[68]

Though submarine crews respect knowledge, they are still human beings and humans will never care how much a leader knows until they know how much he cares. "Great leaders are responsible for creating work environments in which people care about each other, share pride in a common goal, and celebrate the successes of all. For this atmosphere to flourish, we have to realize that, though we can't change everyone around us, we can change ourselves, and make a difference."[69] Developing this atmosphere requires an inordinate amount of effort on the part of the new leader, especially if he is coming into a command that has an oppressive environment. It can be done though. It must be done. By doing this, we will change the idea that "leadership means influencing the community to follow the leader's vision" to "leadership means influencing the community to face its problems."[70]

360 Degree Review

One change that I propose to help leaders foster servant leadership and prevent the toxic leaders from progressing is implementing a 360 degree review process. This is the process by which subordinates have the opportunity to rate their leaders. Admittingly, there is an inherent danger in this type of process since it can have the effect of creating leaders that are more concerned with making friends than accomplishing the mission. It inherently possesses a risk of becoming a popularity contest. If the review system is set up correctly and the evaluation marks are based upon leadership traits and competency, the concern of keeping the people-pleaser leaders can be removed. To be a successful servant leader, there is no requirement to be liked for ones personality.

This 360 degree review process must remove the popularity factor from the equation. Instead, it should focus on capabilities; leadership, tactical, and technical. The method of rating a superior officer will need to be an area of focused research to ensure that superior rating's reflect their true capabilities as a leader and not his ability to make friends or become popular. History has shown that a 360 degree review process has been successfully implemented by several U.S. corporations, increasing productivity, retention and workplace environment. By receiving honest feedback through a 360 degree review process, leaders will be able to see how they are leading from the most important individuals, the people they lead.

Changing the Command Progression

The significant problems we face cannot be solved at the same level of thinking we were at when

we created them

Albert Einstein

With the increasing technological capabilities and complexities of nuclear submarines and their tactical systems, the amount of information that must be mastered to expertly employ them is surpassing the capacity of most officers. Many submarine officers feel that they are becoming a jack of all trades and master of none. The model for officer selection and progression that we use today is the same as the one that Admiral Rickover established. The one change that has been made is a reduction in sea tour lengths for junior officers, department heads, and executive officers.[71] The average reduction in time has been six months per sea tour. This year and a half combined reduction over a career has not affected the nuclear technical ability of the officers, but the tactical ability. It is in that last six months as a junior officer that he learns the most about tactics, ship control and employment. Likewise, it is the last six months as a department head and executive officer that tactics are ingrained. The result is the loss in tactical experience of those that are rising to the ranks of command. The justification for decreasing the tour lengths is to allow more of our senior officers the ability to fill the ranks of admiral and key positions for submarine force relevancy.[72] This is understandable given the battles that take place in the Pentagon for funding. The cost though to the submarine force has been our overall tactical ability. Times and technology have changed and it is time to evaluate whether that same officer career progression process is optimizing the talent we bring into the submarine officer corps.

Why then do we continue with the same model of officer qualification and progression when the work load and knowledge requirements have increased over the years? Then answer is that we have always done it that way since that is the way Admiral Rickover set up the program. As stated earlier, submarine officers qualify first as nuclear officers and then qualify as tactical officers. Why do we do this? It is so the officer of the deck, who has complete control of the submarine, will understand everything that can go wrong and the implications of his actions on the entire ship. Is it possible to be a good officer of the deck and not be nuclear qualified then? The answer is yes. In unique cases on Trident submarines, the Assistant Weapons Officer, is allowed to qualify officer of the deck submerged. He is generally a limited duty officer (LDO) who will never have the opportunity to serve as a senior officer on submarines. Two separate Assistant Weapons Officers on my first submarine qualified officer of the deck and mastered the procedures for reactor plant casualties that would affect them as officers of the deck and then focused on their tactical ability. The result was that they were better officers of the deck than most of the junior officers and department heads. The reason that they were able to do this was due to a capable Engineering Officer of the Watch (EOOW) that stood watch over the reactor and propulsion plants.   If the nuclear reactor can be maintained, as it has since the birth of nuclear submarines, with a competent EOOW, why not split the submarine officer corps forward and aft?

I propose we do just that. Change the submarine officer career path. Establish a pipeline that trains engineering officers specifically to operate the reactor and propulsion plant and a pipeline that trains tactical officers that will master submarine employment. This is not a radical new idea that is untested. The British have employed that model for years with success. This would not change submarine officer manning requirements since we could designate five junior officers as tactical and five as technical. The technical officers would continue their progression as nuclear officers with the opportunity to serve as different division officers during each sea tour, culminating with Engineer as the capstone position. Tactical officers would follow the progression as division officer, department head, executive officer, and then commanding officer.

How then would we address the congressional requirement that every commanding officer be nuclear qualified? In the same manner that we do for commanding officers of nuclear powered aircraft carriers. Each aircraft carrier CO is required to be a pilot first and then nuclear qualified. With the knowledge and experience to fulfill both career paths, it would be impossible to do that concurrently. Thus, when a pilot that has progressed through the ranks to command is selected, he or she is then sent to nuclear power school and prototype for a year prior to assuming command to receive a nuclear certification. This same model could be applied to the tactical officer that is selected for command, thus allowing him to focus solely on tactical employment of the submarine for his entire career until he is ready to assume command. This would allow the technical corps of officers to become more knowledgeable in reactor plant and propulsion plant details, thus making them better advisors to the commanding officer on matters related to plant operations.

Are there risks involved? Yes. Overbearing COs may not take good recommendations or make poor decisions with respect to the nuclear reactor since their level of knowledge will not match that of today's COs. This is where a focus on servant leadership will help to mitigate that risk, training COs to listen more and remove overbearing characteristics. Additionally, submarine Engineers are trained to obey sound judgment and knowledge with respect to plant operations. Operating the plant in a manner or taking any action that would place the crew or submarine in jeopardy would constitute an unlawful order. Next, in a force that gives respect based on knowledge, criticism of the commanding officer may arise among the nuclear trained officers and sailors since his experience and level of knowledge may not match theirs. Once again, if servant leadership is employed properly, the commanding officer will earn the respect of the entire crew.

Conclusion

"It is hard to imagine successful integration of submarines into the operational picture without officers that have an understanding of the principles of operational warfare."[73] "If the Submarine Service is to succeed in the future the Junior Warfare Officer must be provided with the following during individual training: The ability to develop leadership skills, a firm base of knowledge of warfare and strategy, and a foundation of operational experience."[74] This cannot be done with the current rate of increasing information that the junior officer must master to effectively employ the submarine. Nor will we retain the quantity and quality of officers needed to ensure we maintain the premier submarine force without a change in leadership focus. The most effective way to overcome both of these problems is through a combined solution; split the submarine officer career progression and designate tactical officers and engineering officers, and change the leadership training continuum to ingrain servant leadership into the hearts and minds of every officer.

Admiral Rickover realized the importance of having total responsibility. He once said: "Responsibility is a unique concept: it can only reside and inhere (sic) in a single individual. You may share it with others, but your portion is not diminished. You may delegate it, but it is still with you. You may disclaim it, but you cannot divest yourself of it. Even if you do not recognize it or admit its presence, you cannot escape it. If responsibility is rightfully yours, no evasion, or ignorance, or passing the blame can shift the burden to someone else. Unless you can point your finger at the person who is responsible when something goes wrong, then you have never had anyone really responsible."[75] We, as submarine officers, are responsible for the direction that the United States submarine force takes over the next several decades. The responsibility lies with us to make the changes now that will ensure that we are the most

25

operationally proficient, both tactically and technically. The most effective way for this to happen is through a focus on servant-leadership.

Notes

[1] Science Applications International Corporation, "Metamorphosis," 1-10

[2] Ibid, 1-11

[3] Daigle, Enhancing Submarine Operational Relevance, 8

[4] Ibid, 10

[5] Rockwell, *The Rickover Effect*, 39

[6] Blair, "The Man in Tempo," 1

[7] Hinkle, *United States Submarines*, 179

[8] House, *Admiral F.L. Bowman Statement Before House Committee on Science 29 OCTOBER 2003*, 3

[9] Analytic Technologies, "Interview by Diane Sawyer with Admiral Rickover," http://www.analytictech.com/mb021/rickover.htm(accessed 3 November 2008)

[10] House, *Admiral F.L. Bowman Statement Before House Committee on Science 29 OCTOBER 2003*, 2

[11] Ibid, 2

[12] Reed, "Toxic Leadership," 67

[13] Perry, "Ocean's Depths Demand Decisions Like No Others," http://articles.latimes.com/2001/mar/04/news/mn-33222 (accessed 16 November 2008)

[14] House, *Admiral F.L. Bowman Statement Before House Committee on Science 29 OCTOBER 2003*, 3

[15] Navy Personnel Command, "Community Status Brief," http://www.npc.navy.mil/Officer/SubmarineNuclear/(accessed 12 November 2008)

[16] House, *Admiral F.L. Bowman Statement Before House Committee on Science 29 OCTOBER 2003*, 5

[17] Common term in the submarine force for the reactor safety keys and permission to operate the reactor.

[18] House, *Admiral F.L. Bowman Statement Before House Committee on Science 29 OCTOBER 2003*, 2

[19] Navy official Web site. "Perisher, Submarine Command Training in the Royal Navy."

[20] Daigle, Enhancing Submarine Operational Relevance, 5

[21] Casciano, "What Makes a Good CO," United States Naval Institute Proceedings, http://www.usni.org/magazines/proceedings/archive/story.asp? STORY_ID=353 (accessed 6 October 2008)

[22] Ryan, Naval Operations Manpower & Personnel, http://www.navy.mil/navydata/testimony/personnel/recruit0224.txt (accessed 7 January 2008)

[23] Navy First Class Petty Officer Forum, http://www.navyadvancement.com/navy-news/index.php?showtopic=531 (accessed 9 October 2008).

[24] Navy Leadership Continuum, "Officer Leadership Development Continuum," https://www.netc.navy.mil/leadcon_2.html (accessed 5 November 2008)

[25] From personal experience and comments of several submarine officers

[26] Junior Officer Resignation letters, http://www.newnavy.us/naval-resignation-letter.htm (accessed 13 November 2008)

Notes

[27] Ramsey, "Submarine Leadership," http://www.dodccrp.org/files/MF_R_Ramsey.pdf (accessed 12 November 2008)

[28] Ibid

[29] Junior Officer Resignation letters, http://www.newnavy.us/naval-resignation-letter.htm (accessed 13 November 2008)

[30] Ibid

[31] LeFrere, An Assessment of U.S. Navy Junior Officer Retention, 7

[32] Ricks, "A Skipper's Chance to Run a Trident Sub Hits Stormy Waters," The Wall Street Journal

[33] Navy Standard Integrated Personnel System, Navy Monitoring Retention System, https://nsips.nmci.navy.mil/ (accessed 2 January 2008)

[34] Ryan, Naval Operations Manpower & Personnel, http://www.navy.mil/navydata/testimony/personnel/recruit0224.txt (accessed 7 January 2008)

[35] Navy Standard Integrated Personnel System, "Navy Monitoring Retention System," https://nsips.nmci.navy.mil/ (accessed 2 January 2008)

[36] LeFrere, "An Assessment of U.S. Navy Junior Officer Retention." 7

[37] Navy Personnel Command, "Community Status Brief," http://www.npc.navy.mil/Officer/SubmarineNuclear/(accessed 12 November 2008)

[38] Ibid

[39] Ibid

[40] Navy Standard Integrated Personnel System, "Navy Monitoring Retention System," https://nsips.nmci.navy.mil/ (accessed 2 January 2008)

[41] Reed, "Toxic Leadership," 67

[42] Ibid, 68

[43] Ibid, 68

[44] Ibid, 68

[45] Ibid, 68

[46] Tilghman, "Boomer CO fired after first deployment," http://www.navytimes.com/news/2008/12/navy_firedskipper_123008/ (accessed 18 January 2009)

[47] Ibid

[48] Ricks, "A Skipper's Chance to Run a Trident Sub Hits Stormy Waters," The Wall Street Journal

[49] Ibid, A1

[50] Ibid, A1

[51] Ibid, A1

[52] Ibid, A1

[53] Ibid, A6

[54] Ibid, A6

[55] Ibid, A6

[56] Ibid, A6

[57] Daigle, Enhancing Submarine Operational Relevance, 10

[58] Junior Officer Resignation letters, http://www.newnavy.us/naval-resignation-letter.htm (accessed 13 November 2008)

Notes

[59] Wheatley, *Leadership and the new science: Learning about organizations from an orderly universe*, 25

[60] Greenleaf, *The Servant as Leader*, 27

[61] Landry, "Servant-Leadership, Building of Community, and POWs," 6

[62] Ruschman, *Servant-Leadership and the Best Companies to Work for in America*, 123

[63] Spears, *Focus on Leadership*,4

[64] Spears, *Focus on Leadership*,13

[65] Beazley and Beggs, *Teaching Servant Leadership,* 61

[66] Ibid, 61

[67] DePree, *Servant-Leadership: Three Things Necessary*, 91

[68] Beazley and Beggs, *Teaching Servant Leadership,* 61

[69] Ruschman, "Servant-Leadership and the Best Companies to Work for in America," 133

[70] Heifetz, *Leadership without easy answers*, 14

[71] Navy Personnel Command, "Community Status Brief," http://www.npc.navy.mil/Officer/SubmarineNuclear/(accessed 12 November 2008)

[72] Ibid

[73] Daigle, Enhancing Submarine Operational Relevance, 7

[74] Ramsey, "Submarine Leadership," http://www.dodccrp.org/files/MF_R_Ramsey.pdf (accessed 12 November 2008)

[75] House, *Admiral F.L. Bowman Statement Before House Committee on Science 29 OCTOBER 2003*, 6

Bibliography

Analytic Technologies, "Interview by Diane Sawyer with Admiral Rickover," http://www.analytictech.com/mb021/rickover.htm(accessed 3 November 2008)

Blair, Clay, Jr. "The Man in Tempo," Time, 11 January 1954.

Beazley, Hamilton and Julie Beggs. Teaching Servant-leadership. In Spears, L. & Lawrence, M. (Ed.), Focus on Leadership: servant-leadership for the 21st century. (pp. ix xii.). New York: John Wiley & Sons. Inc. 2002

Casciano, Emil, Marc Elsensohn, Istein Jensen, Dermot Mulholland, John Richardson, and Ian Salter. "What Makes a Good CO." United States Naval Institute Proceedings 131, no. 4 (April 2005). http://www.usni.org/magazines/proceedings/archive/story.asp? STORY_ID=353 (accessed 6 October 2008).

Daigle, LCDR Michael J. Jr. Enhancing Submarine Operational Relevance. Research Report. Newport, RI: Naval War College. 2008.

DePree, Max. *Servant-Leadership: Three Things Necessary*. In Spears, L. & Lawrence, M. (Ed.), Focus on Leadership: servant-leadership for the 21st century. (pp. ix xii.). New York: John Wiley & Sons. Inc. 2002.

Dobbs, Michael J. How the Twig was Bent: Developing Young Bubble Heads for the Challenges of Command. United States Naval Proceedings 133, no. 6 (June 2007).

Greenleaf, R. K. *The Servant as Leader*. Cambridge, Mass.: Center for Applied Studies, 1973.

Heifetz, R. A. *Leadership without easy answers*. Cambridge, MA: Belknap Press, 1994.

Hinkle, David Randall, Harry Harrison Caldwell, Arne C. Johnson, Naval Submarine League (U.S.), *United States Submarines*, Published by Naval Submarine League, Southport, Conn.: Hugh Lauter Levin; Lancaster: Gazelle 2002.

Junior Officer Resignation letters. http://www.newnavy.us/naval-resignation-letter.htm (accessed 13 November 2008).

Kotter, John P. Leading Change. Boston, MA: Harvard Business School Press, 1996.

Landry, Brian W. "Servant-Leadership, Building of Community, and POWs." International Journal for Servant-Leadership, vol 4 (November 2008): 217-232.

LeFrere, Kerwin J. "An Assessment of U.S. Navy Junior Officer Retention." Research Report no. A241704. Maxwell AFB, AL: Air Command and Staff College, 2005.

Mack, Stephen. "Perisher: Submarine Command Training in the Royal Navy." Undersea Warfare, Spring 2003. http://www.navy.mil/ navydata/cno/n87/usw/issue_18/ perisher.htm (accessed 11 November 2008).

Navy Center for Personal and Professional Development. "Career Progression." https://www.netc.navy.mil/centers/cppd/ (accessed 18 November 2008).

Navy First Class Forum. http://www.navyadvancement.com/navy-news/index.php?showtopic=531 (accessed 9 October 2008).

Navy Leadership Continuum. "Officer Leadership Development Continuum." https://www.netc.navy.mil/leadcon_2.html (accessed 5 November 2008).

Navy official Web site. "Perisher, Submarine Command Training in the Royal Navy." http://www.navy.mil/navydata/cno/n87/usw/issue_18/perisher.htm (accessed 16 January 2009).

Navy Personnel Command. "Community Status Brief." http://www.npc.navy.mil/Officer/SubmarineNuclear/(accessed 12 November 2008).

Navy Standard Integrated Personnel System. "Navy Monitoring Retention System." https://nsips.nmci.navy.mil/ (accessed 2 January 2008).

Perry, Tony. "Ocean's Depths Demand Decisions Like No Others." Los Angeles Times, 4 March 2001. http://articles.latimes.com/2001/mar/04/news/mn-33222(accessed 16 November 2008).

Ramsey, Lt Cdr RN Ryan. "Submarine Leadership." N74 Submarine Development Squadron 12. http://www.dodccrp.org/files/MF_R_Ramsey.pdf (accessed 12 November 2008).

Reed, Colonel George E. Toxic Leadership. Military Review, July-August 2004, 67.

Reilly, Gregory D. How Tactical Experience Affects Confidence About Combat Decision Making. Fort Leavenworth, KS: U.S. Army Command and General Staff College, 1997.

Ricks, Thomas E. "A Skipper's Chance to Run a Trident Sub Hits Stormy Waters," The Wall Street Journal, November 20, 1997, Al,A6.

Rockwell, Theodore. The Rickover Effect: How One Man Made a Difference, iUniverse, 2002.

Ruschman, Nancy L. "Servant-Leadership and the Best Companies to Work for in America." In Spears, L. & Lawrence, M. (Ed.), *Focus on Leadership: servant-leadership for the 21st century*. (pp. ix xii.). New York: John Wiley & Sons. Inc. 2002.

Ryan, N. R. Jr., Vice Admiral. Naval Operations Manpower & Personnel, http://www.navy.mil/navydata/testimony/personnel/recruit0224.txt (accessed 7 January 2008).

Spears, L. C. & Lawrence, M. (Ed.). *Focus on Leadership: servant-leadership for the 21st century*. New York: John Wiley & Sons, 2002.

Science Applications International Corporation. "Metamorphosis." http://www.saic.com/news/ (accessed October 11, 2008).

Tilghman, Andrew. "Boomer CO fired after first deployment." Navy Times, 2 January 2009. http://www.navytimes.com/news/2008/12/navy_firedskipper_123008/ (accessed 18 January 2009).

US House. *Statement of Admiral F.L. Bowman Before the House Committed on Science 29 OCTOBER 2003*," http://history.nasa.gov/columbia/Troxell/Columbia%20Web%20Site/ Documents/Congress/House/OCTOBE~1/Bowman%20Opening%20Statement.pdf (accessed 18 December 2008).

Wheatley, M. J. Leadership and the new science: Learning about organizations from an orderly universe. San Francisco, CA: Barret-Koehler, 1994.

www.ingramcontent.com/pod-product-compliance
Lightning Source LLC
Chambersburg PA
CBHW081804280526
45789CB00008B/2989